The Land Mogul's Playbook for Social Media Ads

The Land Mogul's Playbook for Social Media Ads

How to Sell Your Land in Record Time

by

John Alexander

NuDay Publishing

Author's and Publisher's Legal Claims and Legal Disclaimers and Disclosures

ISBN: 9798391711902

Copyright © 2023 Alexander All Rights Reserved

Legal Disclosures

"This publication is designed to provide accurate and authoritative information in regard to the subject matter covered. It is sold with the understanding that the publisher is not engaged in rendering legal, accounting or other professional service. If legal advice or other expert assistance is required, the services of a competent professional person should be sought." From a Declaration of Principles jointly adopted by a committee of the American Bar Association and a committee of publishers and associations.

Results from use of the information may vary and may result in a total loss of your advertising dollars spent. Do not use this material unless you can accept the possible loss of 100% of your advertising capital.

Copyright/Reproduction Information and Permissions for reprints may be requested from the Publisher

Trademark Disclosures:

"Facebook" and "Facebook Marketplace" and "Facebook Ads Manager: and "Instagram" are registered trademarks of Facebook, Inc. and its use in the book does not imply endorsement or affiliation with the company.

"Google" is a trademark of Google LLC. and its use in the book does not imply endorsement or affiliation with the company.

"YouTube" is a trademark of Google LLC. And its use in the book does not imply endorsement or affiliation with the company.

"Go High Level" is a registered trademark of High Level Marketing LLC and its use in the book or other writing does not imply endorsement or affiliation with the company.

Contents
Introduction
Marketplace Ads will go out to both Facebook and Instagram.
Learn About Flipping Land for Free
How to Market and Sell a Property on Facebook with or without Seller Financing Options
Marketing a Property on Facebook
Step 1: Research Competitors' Ads Before creating your listing.
Step 2: Create a New Listing
Step 3: Mention Seller Financing Options (if applicable)
Step 4: Monitor and Optimize Your Listing
Crafting a Compelling Land Listing: Using Clarity and Cultural Nuances
Crafting the Million Dollar Ad
The Right Google Map to Use
Accessing the Facebook Ads Manager
What never to Include in the Ad
Magic Words in your Ad
Key Landmark or Feature
Boosting Your Ad to access thousands of buyers
My Secret Boosting Process
Join local Buy/Sell Groups for more Reach
Summary
RESOURCES
Books by John Alexander
About the Author

INTRODUCTION

Don't make the mistakes I did when I started advertising land on Facebook!...

I wasted a ton of ad dollars until I figured it out!...

A simple and affordable way to make Facebook algorithms work for you!...

Learn the secrets of creating the perfect land ad for Facebook Marketplace!

I have been a real estate investor for over 40 years, I've gone from advertising land in Newspaper classified ads to today's latest methods. And I'm excited to share how my students and I are using Facebook Marketplace to sell our land flips, both for cash and with owner financing.

In today's digital age, advertising properties on online platforms like Facebook Marketplace has become increasingly popular and effective. In this book, we'll guide you through the process of creating a compelling and successful advertisement using a real live example of land I listed and sold on Facebook Marketplace.

I list all my land flips on Facebook Marketplace and in this book, I'll show you exactly how we do it to get our land sold fast and at top price.

From crafting the right title and category to properly organizing photos, boosting visibility, and ensuring compliance with Facebook's housing regulations.

Marketplace Ads will go out to both Facebook and Instagram.

Land doesn't really fall under the House For Sale category and needs a special placement to get looking right. That's where this book comes into play.

I use a different method than the normal House or House for Rent category in marketplace ad. Marketplace ads for real estate are mainly tailored for home sales and rentals, and they don't have a format for land. However, I have developed a process to get around that problem, which I will detail as we cover all the essential steps to help you generate leads and, ultimately, close the sale. Get ready to master the art of online land advertising on Facebook!

Learn About Flipping Land for Free

Join my FREE Facebook Group to learn more about Flipping Land at https://facebook.com/groups/landmogul/

"Facebook" and "Facebook Marketplace" and "Facebook Ads Manager: and "Instagram" are registered trademarks of Facebook, Inc. and its use in the book does not imply endorsement or affiliation with the company.

HOW TO MARKET AND SELL A PROPERTY ON FACEBOOK WITH OR WITHOUT SELLER FINANCING OPTIONS

In this short book, we will explore how to effectively market and sell a property on Facebook. This method has taken me years to perfect and I hope it will save you time in helping you sell your land faster by building off my methods detailed within these pages.

We will also discuss the option of seller financing for vacant land and whether it is advisable to allow buyers to make improvements on the property before they fully own it.

Marketing a Property on Facebook

We will use a live example of some property I recently sold on the marketplace and it will better demonstrate the process of listing property there.

The goal is to create an attractive and effective ad that captures the attention of potential buyers.

Step 1: Research Competitors' Ads Before creating your listing.

It's important to research competitors' ads to get a better understanding of the market and gather useful ideas. To do this, go to Facebook Marketplace and search for similar properties in the area using keywords like "land for sale," "owner financing," in the name of the city or county where your land is located. Analyze the ads to identify successful strategies or avoidable mistakes that can help improve your own listing.

Step 2: Create a New Listing

Once you have a good grasp of the competition, head to Facebook Marketplace and click on "Create a New Listing." Select the "Item for Sale" icon. This is the first secret to selling land on the Marketplace. We don't use the Home for Sale or Rent Icon.

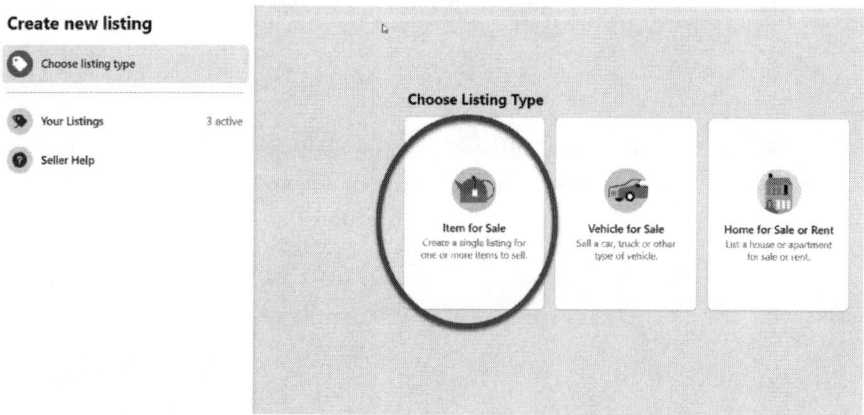

Next, fill in the required information about your property, such as location, price, and details. In the Category Section, you will want to select "Miscellaneous", finally select New as the condition.

Make sure to use high-quality photos that showcase the best features of your property and write a detailed, engaging description that highlights its unique selling points.

Step 3: Mention Seller Financing Options (if applicable)

If you're offering seller financing options, make sure to say this in your ad. Example: "Owner will Finance." This can be an attractive feature for potential buyers who may not have the cash to pay upfront or who are looking for more flexible payment terms.

Do not detail any of the financing terms, down payment, and monthly payment amounts, or you could be in violation of Federal legal credit requirements. Even mentioning 10% down is a violation without full disclosures along with this statement. Never mention any of the terms of the loan other than the price. If done wrong, you can also get your Facebook account suspended if it gets flagged for credit violations.

You simply should give these details as it becomes something buyers will need to contact you about. They typically start by asking about the down payment to make sure it's even a possibility for them to buy. This gets the conversation by messenger going and is the perfect subject to start the process.

Step 4: Monitor and Optimize Your Listing

After your listing is live, it's crucial to monitor its performance and respond to inquiries from potential buyers promptly. Engage with interested parties, answer their questions, and provide additional information about the property when needed.

Regularly review your listing's performance to identify areas of improvement and make necessary adjustments to optimize its visibility and effectiveness. To find these metrics, click into marketplace/selling and click on your ad. It will have the following link called "Insights" that will give you those numbers. To find a buyer, you need the CLICK ON LISTINGS numbers to be in the hundreds.

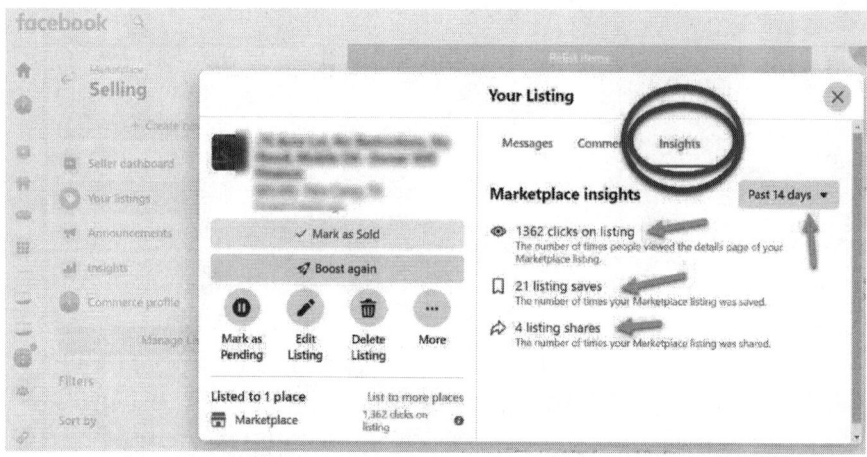

Step 5: Share Your Listing on social media and Relevant Groups

To increase the reach of your property listing, share it on your personal Facebook profile, as well as on relevant Facebook groups where potential buyers may be browsing for properties. Look for local real estate groups, investment clubs, or community forums where your target audience is likely to be active. Sharing your listing in these groups can help attract more potential buyers and generate greater interest in your property.

I recently did a Zoom Training Session on this topic and gave it away for free to anyone buying this book!

**Watch the Free Reply here:
https://johnalexander.com/marketplace**

or scan this QR Code and Watch it Now!

~John Alexander~

CRAFTING A COMPELLING LAND LISTING: USING CLARITY AND CULTURAL NUANCES

Creating an effective land listing requires a balance of clarity and cultural understanding. It's essential to avoid sounding too much like a corporate sales pitch, as people are more likely to engage with ads that feel personal and genuine. A touch of authenticity in your ad can go a long way in attracting potential buyers.

In certain cultures, such as Spanish-speaking communities, specific terms can be used to convey the nature of the transaction. For instance, using "Dueño a Dueño" (owner to owner) indicates that the sale is between two private individuals and not involving banks or third parties.

This term can be particularly useful when offering owner financing options. Similarly, "en pagos" (in payments) implies that the land is for sale with payment plans available.

When crafting your ad, it's crucial to use clear language that communicates the details of the sale effectively. In Spanish, "Terreno en Venta" (Land for sale) is a commonly used phrase that indicates a cash transaction is preferred.

It's essential to remember that discussing owner financing or "Dueño a Dueño" arrangements should be where the initial conversation goes when responding to buyers as they contact you via Messenger directly from the ad.

Crafting the Million Dollar Ad

When deciding what information to include in your listing, consider the location of the property. While it's not necessary to provide the exact location, it's a good idea to offer a general idea of where the land is situated.

It's rare I actually have a picture of the land itself as in the first picture below, as I usually never visit the land. Every part of the sale is done on my laptop and phone.

Here are the typical type pictures I use for all my land ads. Grab them from Google Maps or a GIS website. Mark them up using a screen saver apps. There are many free apps for graphics. I mainly use just arrows, circles, text, and lines to create these so any basic app should work fine. I have used Snagit™ by Techsmith.com for many years.

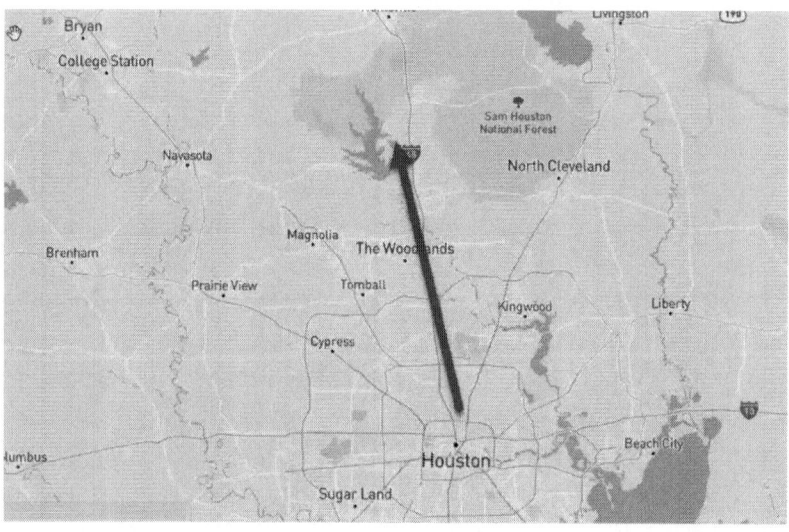

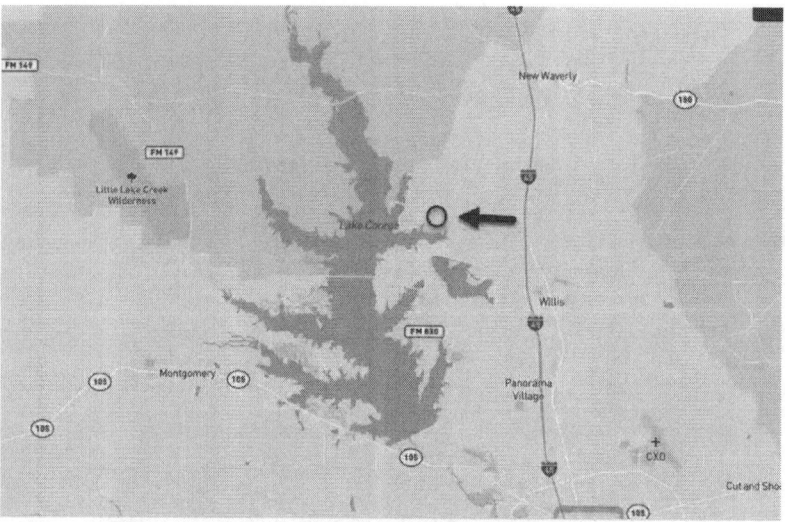

I make sure in my street map views that the major city is referenced so buyer can see how far the travel time is and where it sits in reference to where they live, which is often, that major city.

A landmark such as This Lake is also a great picture as it shows exactly where on the lake, the lot sits.

Land Mogul's Playbook for Social Media Ads   21

As we zoom in, switch to the satellite view to show the lay of the land, so to speak. Number of houses etc. show up, and then the actual neighborhood is seen in the fully zoomed screenshot. This is a key selling picture that should be the featured picture in the ad.

It's going to allow people to walk the area using the features they see in the picture to narrow down exactly where and how the land sits on that street.

This can be achieved by sharing maps or pictures of the area, giving potential buyers a sense of the property's surroundings. More specific directions or coordinates can be provided later in the conversation if the buyer expresses further interest.

The Right Google Map to Use

I also include a custom-made map with driving directions mapped out in a "Google® My Places" map. There are plenty of Youtube® videos showing you how to create these. I will also use the line feature in this map to draw out the property lines.

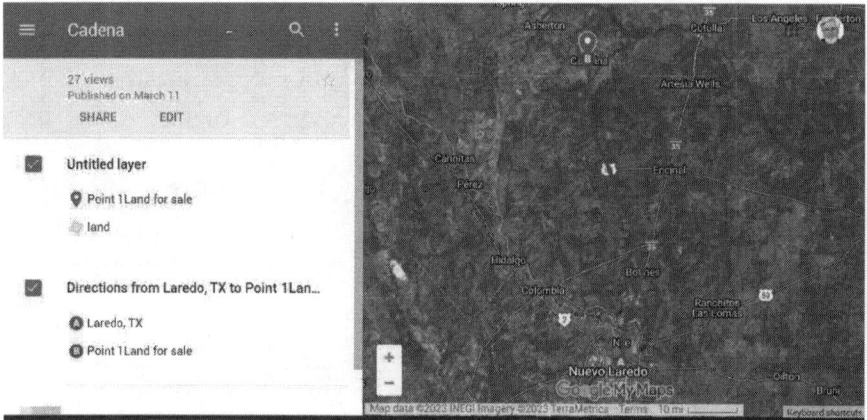

Create the map, then use the shared link to provide your buyer leads when the location or address is asked for. Notice, I never include this or the address in the ad. This is another "part" of the conversation once a lead starts messaging you.

Accessing the Facebook Ads Manager

It's also important to immediately open the Facebook Ads Manager and select the HOUSING category under the Special Ad

Categories. To access the Ad's Manager, simply type in Facebook Ads Manager" in a new browser window and it should take you directly to your Account manager. Then click on CAMPAIGN, then on the Title of your Ad, then click the Edit button below the title. This brings you to the area where you will scroll down until you find the following Special Ad Categories selection.

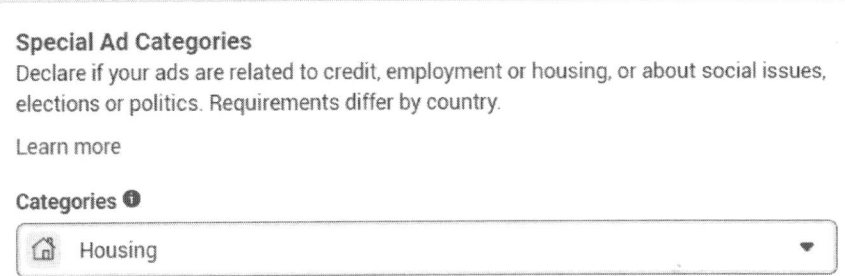

Select the HOUSING category in the dropdown window. Then in the bottom right of the page, select PUBLISH AD.

If you miss this important set, Facebook will DENY your ad. It must be completed or your ad will not show up in the Markplace.

What never to Include in the Ad

Earlier, I discussed not going into details in the ad about the financing details. Here is a more detailed explanation about why and further if you did want to include them (which is not a good idea from a marketing stand point) here is how to properly list payment details.

When creating a financing ad for the sale of property, it's important to be aware of credit laws that prohibit certain practices. One thing that should never be addressed in a financing ad is partial loan terms without listing all of them, including the Annual Percentage Rate (APR).

The Truth in Lending Act (TILA) requires lenders to disclose the APR and all other loan terms to potential borrowers. This means that in a financing ad for the sale of property, it is illegal to list only part of the loan terms without including the APR and other relevant information. Failing to do so could result in legal penalties and damage to your reputation as a seller. Even mentioning a percentage down payment as in... "10% down" will trigger this legal issue. However, using words like "Small Down" or "Owner will Finance" is fine to use in ads.

In addition, it's important to avoid making any false or misleading statements in your financing ad. This includes misrepresenting the terms of the loan or making promises that you cannot keep. Doing so could also result in legal and financial consequences.

To ensure compliance with credit laws and to maintain a good reputation as a seller, it's important to work with a licensed and reputable mortgage broker or lender who can assist you in creating a financing ad that meets all legal requirements and accurately represents the terms of the loan.

If you do offer owner financing, make sure you are not using an interest rate that is above your state's maximum for consumers. Only licensed lenders can offer higher-than-normal rates, or commercial loans that are outside the normal consumer credit regulations. Seek the advice of an attorney in the state where the property is located before making lending offers.

MAGIC WORDS IN YOUR AD

Keep in mind the importance of authenticity, using familiar terms and phrases where applicable to establish a connection with your target audience.

When it comes to describing the property, make sure to highlight its unique features, benefits, and any relevant information that may entice prospective buyers. High-quality photos or videos of the land can further enhance the appeal of your listing, providing visual evidence of the property's potential.

Maintaining an open and responsive communication channel with interested parties is also crucial.

Address any questions or concerns they may have promptly and provide additional details when needed. This attentiveness demonstrates your commitment to the sale and helps build trust with potential buyers.

By following these guidelines, you can create a compelling ad that effectively attracts and engages potential buyers, increasing the likelihood of a successful land sale.

When filling out the Details in the Ad, use some key items like Size of the frontage and depth of the land. If it has no restrictions, that's a big plus, so add that. If it has no HOA, add that too. Here's what I used on this example property:

Title:
Double Lot near Lake Conroe, Mobile Homes OK, Will Owner Finance

Location and Price Boxes: In the ad, I priced it at $60,000, the property falls under the miscellaneous category and is listed in new condition.

Description:
Discover the Perfect Weekend Getaway: Double Lot near Lake Conroe.
Nestled near Lake Conroe, this double lot offers endless possibilities for those seeking a weekend retreat or a cozy place to call home. With a little over 4,000 square feet, the property is suitable for a mobile home, a tiny house, or even a custom-built residence, thanks to its unique configuration. 60 ft frontage by 140 ft Deep
.

The community surrounding the property boasts a range of amenities, including a swimming pool, perfect for cooling off during hot summer days. Moreover, its proximity to Houston – just an hour's drive away – makes it an ideal escape from the bustling city life.

Whether you're looking to park your RV for weekend trips or build a small, comfortable home, this double lot provides a versatile canvas for you to explore your dreams.

Try NOT to make your ad sound like a real estate agent wrote it. Avoid flowery language, don't exaggerate, don't hide the problems either. If it is in a flood zone, say it somewhere in the description.

You will find that most people don't even read the description, they are contacting you off the pictures and headline. You will often have to answer their questions in your messenger conversation which are address in the description. This tells you they don't read it. That's ok, be patient, some can't even find the button to open the description so just go with it and give answer the question without referring them back to the ad.

KEY LANDMARK OR FEATURE

Remember to focus on the lot's most prominent assets and provide a concise, engaging headline to capture the attention of potential buyers. High-quality photos will also help showcase the property's full potential.

When creating your listing, ensure that it reaches the right audience by Boosting it on the platform you're using, such as Facebook Marketplace. Additionally, adjust your ad settings to hide it from your friends, allowing you to target a wider range of potential buyers who may be genuinely interested in the property.

By following these tips, you'll craft an enticing property listing that effectively highlights the unique features of this double lot near Lake Conroe and draws in potential buyers eager to explore its potential.

When uploading pictures to your listing, number them sequentially to ensure they appear in the desired order. Begin with an aerial photo of the double lot, marked with arrows to highlight its unique configuration. Follow this with a zoomed-out image showing the property's proximity to Lake Conroe, emphasizing its easy access to public boat ramps and popular fishing spots.

Continue to showcase the lot's location by including a street map view, illustrating its relation to nearby cities such as Willis, Conroe, and Houston. Use arrows to point out the property's exact location on the map, giving potential buyers a clear understanding of where it lies within the broader context.

BOOSTING YOUR AD TO ACCESS THOUSANDS OF BUYERS

Once you've listed your property on Facebook Marketplace, get a ton of eyes on your ad by Boosting it for greater visibility. Without boosting, expect just hundreds to see your ad, whereas boosting will get thousands seeing it. And these are real buyers too!

My Secret Boosting Process

The second key part of getting your land sold using Facebook Marketplace is Boosting the Ad.

I like to do a $3.00 a day Boost for 3 days during the first part of week starting on Monday. This allows Facebook algorithms to figure out the best buyers to show the ad to for when you will increase your budget for the weekend. You will need to use the Custom Budget link shown below to get to a $3.00 a day ad choice:

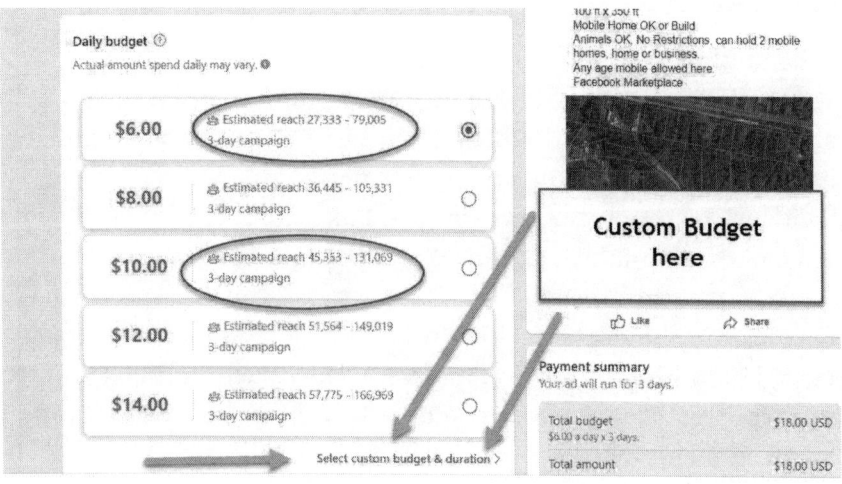

Come back in with a $10 per day for a three-day boost on the weekend. See the above graphic for the details on making this selection. Make sure you are boosting your ad at least every Friday, Saturday, and Sunday until it is sold.

Boosting will get you hundreds or even thousands of more impressions per week depending on the amount you are willing to pay. And these impressions are pushed to land buyer the algorithms have determined are interested in buying land. This kind of advertising is worth every dollar spent.

Renewal Boosts. When you renew your Boost, **YOU WILL get an Error or a Message** from Facebook saying your Ad was Denied. This is because the system creates a new ad inside your Ad account which means you will need to edit this new ad inside your ad the same way you adjusted it the first time you listed it. All Ads under "Item for Sale" are assumed NOT to be real estate so you have to manually turn on the HOUSING disclosure each time you reboost your ad. Simple go the Facebook manager and select "Housing" under the Special Ad Categories section as detailed earlier in this book.

JOIN LOCAL BUY/SELL GROUPS FOR MORE REACH

In addition to boosting your ad, share the same Marketplace ad listing in up to 10 relevant Buy/Sell Groups at a time, maximizing its exposure to potential buyers in the area where the property is located. Keep in mind that if you elect to place it in other Groups, you must not select the Hide it from Friends option as it will not allow you to then show it in Facebook Groups. In order to do this, you first search Facebook for Buy/Sell or Trade Groups.

The best way to find these groups is to add the nearest big city name to your search term, i.e. "Buy/Sell San Antonio TX." Join these groups before you need to sell your land because it can take up to a week or two to get approved to join these groups. Bigger ones, approve membership faster in general.

Sometimes these group demand you live in the area or they will deny you membership. To get by this issue, explain in one of the question boxes that while you don't live in this city full time, you do own a property here and wish to join. This will usually get you in.

Also search for groups that cater to just land sales and join those too.

Once you have joined 10 to 20 of these groups, Facebook lets you post your ad up to 10 of them at a time, so post to your initial 10, then go back in after you posted and published your ad and reopen your listing under the Seller link in the Marketplace and click on the View Listing link and follow to this drop-down box:

This will allow you to list in another 10 groups at a time. Rinse and repeat until you have listed it in all the groups you feel you want to list the ad in.

SUMMARY

To successfully advertise land on Facebook Marketplace, create a well-organized description highlighting key features such as versatility, location, and utilities. Upload photos of the land via Google Maps or GIS and photos that showcase the property's proximity to a city, lake or other main reason for them wanting to buy in that location.

Use the **Items for Sale** selection rather than the **Homes** icon to create your ad. Pictures and Headlines is what get leads reacting and following up with you. All Ads under "Item for Sale" are assumed NOT to be real estate so you have to manually turn on the HOUSING disclosure each time you place your ad under this section.

Join relevant buy-sell groups to increase visibility, and consider boosting the ad with a budget of $10 per day or more for optimal lead generation using my secret Boost Formula explained above.

Finally, ensure the ad is categorized as "Housing" in Facebook Ads Manager to avoid disapproval due to housing-related requirements.

Much caution should be used when using Owner Financing in ads. If you do use such terms in the ad, follow the guideline we covered as well as laws, statutes, and guidance of both state and federal regulatory agencies. I learned through trial and error that it is far better from a marketing aspect to only announce you can offer owner financing in an ad, which is the Lead part of the process; then deal with the terms etc., as part of the prospecting and qualification that comes later in the sales process.

The Marketplace is an amazing place to sell land. It's fast to create the ad, it is controllable by boosting it. It teaches itself how to find better buyers using algorithms and it is easy to manage conversations with buyers.

I hope to meet you in our Land Mogul Facebook Group soon. Check below for the link.

I recently did a Zoom Training Session on this topic and gave it away for free to anyone buying this book!

Watch the Free Reply here: https://johnalexander.com/marketplace

or scan this QR Code and Watch it Now!

~John Alexander~

RESOURCES

Join my FREE Facebook Group to learn more about Flipping Land at **https://facebook.com/groups/landmogul**

Use John's Favorite CRM to Explode Your Business!

Agents can host auction details in this system and collect emails, phone calls, and texts from buyers and sellers. Schedule phone appointments and more.
You are now ready to revolutionize your real estate business and stay ahead of the competition? It's time to invest in the cutting-edge CRM system so you can automate much of your business. I have used this next level CRM for the last 2 years and it is so robust, it is currently linking into ChatGPT which will allow you to up your CRM game. It is the ultimate CRM solution for real estate investors like you who want to excel in the fast-paced world of real estate.

You'll have the power to manage every aspect of your real estate business with ease. From hosting websites, to interacting with your social media accounts and DM's, it details and capturing leads to scheduling phone appointments and sending out timely reminders., This top-of-the-line CRM will streamline your processes and help you build stronger relationships with both buyers and sellers.

Imagine having a centralized platform where you can effortlessly collect and manage emails, phone calls, and texts from potential clients, giving you the edge over other agents who are still struggling with piece-milling email systems, texting system, answering service, calendar scheduler, websites and more.

This CRM will save you time, reduce errors, and allow you to focus on what truly matters – providing exceptional service to your clients and closing more deals.

But that's not all. This CRM also offers an array of advanced features that will elevate your real estate business to new heights. Its powerful automation tools and built-in marketing capabilities will help you generate more leads and close deals faster than ever before. Plus, the user-friendly interface and comprehensive reporting features will make it easy for you to track your progress and make data-driven decisions.

Don't let outdated systems hold you back from achieving your full potential. By investing in this CRM, you'll be equipping yourself with the tools you need to become a leader in your market space and secure your place as a top-performing real estate agent.

It's time to level up your real estate business and experience the difference a high-end CRM can make. **Go to the link below** to get started with a free trial and discover the true power of this cutting-edge CRM solution. Your future success in the world of high-bidder auctions is just a few clicks away!

This is my affiliate link and it pays me a small commission and as one of my affiliate members, I want to help you succeed. You can reach out to me on Facebook® or Instagram® DM for occasional help and direction just let me know you are one of my affiliate members.

With this link, you can get a free 14-day trial and test drive it for free. CRM Here: **HTTPS://LEADMACHINEPLUS.COM**

BOOKS BY JOHN ALEXANDER

Available at https://JohnAlexander.com

New Book Release

MASTERING THE 3-DAY HIGHEST-BIDDER SALE FOR REAL ESTATE AGENTS

Sell Your Listings Faster and for More Money in Today's Slowing Market

JOHN ALEXANDER

Amazon

Living Trusts for Real Estate Investors

Stop Exposing Your Name and Assets to Lawsuits and Competition

Corporate entities have their place as liability protection, but they don't protect all the other properties the company may own, and they certainly don't hide what you own and where your properties are located.

It also informs your competition exactly what you are doing, and in what part of the city you found your sweet-spot for great real estate to flip. And if you hold real estate as a long-term investment, as in rentals, you want even more privacy.

You will also learn:
How to conduct your own title searches
How to self-close your own transactions

Who Needs This Book?
Wholesalers
Land Flippers
Landlords-Owners   **Available at Amazon.com**

#59 Amazon Best Seller List

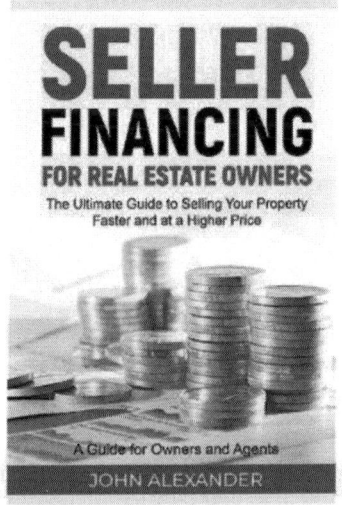

Seller Financing for Real Estate Owners: The...
› John Alexander
Paperback
$12.95

One of my most popular books is "How to Flip Vacant Lots" while it's available on Amazon, by ordering it the link below as an instant download, you will also get access to some training videos and more, while saving money at the Amazon price.

This book will teach you a unique method of using the buyer's money to fund the purchase between you and the seller. This prevents you from having to purchase the land upfront and then hoping you can sell it later at a profit.

Buy it and Down load it at: **https://selffundingflip.com**

ABOUT THE AUTHOR

John Alexander is an active speaker, author and real estate investor of over 40-years and a best-selling author. Past Mortgage Broker and Business Appraiser. He has trained tens of thousands of real estate investors nationally since 1994. He has authored over 15 books on various real estate flipping techniques including the creation and publication of the Flex Option, The Inverse Purchase, introduced the concept of Equitable Ownership to the Industry in 1999, created the Contract Release which gave rise to the Novation method, as well as various creative note buying methods. He holds the trademark Land Mogul®.

www.JohnAlexander.com